MR PEGELOW

AT THE GATES OF HELL

Bob Streblow

Published by
Jubilee Design

1.25

JUBILEE DESIGN
112 Horseshoe Dr.
Burnet, TX 78611-5919
512-756-7321
goodmon@tstar.net

9th Printing 2003

Foreword

The "Vision of Mr. Pegelow" never fails to move me. The first time I heard it was about three months after Bob Streblow had gone through the sinner's prayer with me and led me to Jesus. My shirt collar was never very dirty, nor was I an alcoholic, but I could identify with Mr. Pegelow. I feel a kinship with both these men. I look forward to finding my nameplate at their end of the banquet table.

Orval Sherwood

1

The True Report

You are about to read a true story which happened to me! It is very real! I know before you have finished this book, you may shed a few tears; you may laugh a few times. However, I don't believe you will ever forget my story, for what you are about to read happened as a direct visitation from God. May God make it real to you also as you continue reading.

> *We read in the Old Testament that before David became King, Saul swore an oath to kill him. Because of King Saul's fierce anger and*

jealousy, David was forced to leave his home, family and friends in order to save his own life. He even lived in the land of his enemies until they also desired to kill him. Eventually, he found a great cave and he crawled into it to hide.

In Psalm 142:4, David's distress is apparent: **"I looked on my right hand, and beheld, but there was no man that would know me: refuge failed me; no man cared for my soul."**

Many people feel that no one cares at all what happens to them. They find no help in their personal relationships nor in religious systems, so they try to hide themselves in caves of their own making.

The bottle is a cave for millions of people. Many more seek help in drugs, others through adultery and/or divorce. I could go on and on and on. Perhaps you have sometimes felt no one cares what happens to you, that no one understands you. Perhaps **you** are one of the many millions who suffers from acute loneliness and depression. Perhaps you have often felt you were in a cave and there was no one who really cared.

I am going to tell you about a man who happened across the pathway of my life. He was already a man when I was a boy. Every week, sometimes many times a week, I passed him. I made fun of him; I mocked him; I did many things that probably hurt him.

But one night, July 31, 1951, when I was still a teenager, Jesus Christ set up a roadblock in my life. He stopped me on the road I was traveling — **a dead end street.** He rescued me from an automobile accident by warning me through the Holy Spirit that it was my last chance to accept the grace of God. That night at a revival meeting, I went to the altar and accepted Jesus as my Saviour.

I had attended church all my life but had never been born again. That night I discovered it wasn't enough to be raised in church or in a Christian family. That does not make you a Christian. You must be "born again" (John 3:7).

**"Marvel not that I said unto thee,
Ye must be born again."**

That night I experienced salvation. The Lord apprehended my life. The same evening I received the Baptism in the Holy Spirit.

As I found myself making my way to the altar to surrender my life to Jesus, the five other teenagers who had come to church with me left. They were laughing and making fun of me. One of them was my girlfriend. I was 16 years of age at the time.

My friends drove away from the service in a brand-new Buick car. Five miles from the church they went off the road and down an embankment. They wrapped that brand-new Buick around a big oak tree. My girlfriend was dead on the spot. Another young man, one of my closest friends, was dead. Two others were unconscious. Although injured, one managed to get back to the church, blood coming down the side of his face, tears in his eyes.

Oh, how glad I am that on that night I believed the true report:

"And we know that the Son of God
is come, and hath given us an un-
derstanding, that we may know
him that is true, and we are in him
that is true, even in his Son Jesus
Christ. This is the true God, and
eternal life" (I John 5:20).

The seat in which I usually sat was twisted
beyond belief and wrapped closest to the big
oak tree.

"The life which I now live in the
flesh I live by the faith of the Son of
God who loved me and gave himself
for me" (Galatians 2:20).

It was the goodness of God that led me to
repentance that night. My body would be in a
cemetery, a cold stone marker the only re-
membrance of my life, had I not listened to
the Spirit of God that told me this was my
last chance to get right with Him. Not only
my body but my soul would have forever been
separated from the Spirit of God. I can truly
say, the life I now live I live by the faith of the
Son of God!

When God speaks, it's always best to listen. When God's Spirit comes upon you and convinces you of your need, the Bible says:

"Seek ye the Lord while He may be found, call ye upon Him while He is near" (Isaiah 55:6).

The following warning should be heeded:

"And the Lord said, My spirit shall not always strive with man, for that he also is flesh" (Genesis 6:3).

It is always best to answer when He calls! Believe me, when God speaks, He knows your beginning and He knows your end. When He says to do something, it is time to do it.

That July night which might have been my ending, turned out to be my beginning! I began attending church and revival meetings regularly. Week after week as I passed the Milwaukee Road Depot in my home town, there on the steps was that same old man. He was known as the town wino. His cave was the bottle. His name was **Mr. Pegelow.**

2

The Call

Three weeks after my conversion, I was baptized in water, identifying myself with the death and resurrection of Jesus Christ (Romans 6:4; Colossians 2:12). Three days later God called me to the ministry. I began preparing myself for the ministry by going to Bible College.

About three months into my first year of college, while in Church History Class one day, the Holy Spirit interrupted the class. The Spirit began to move and everyone began to weep. The teacher recognized that God, in His sovereign will, was moving in that class. He stopped teaching, letting the Holy Spirit have His way. Simultaneously, all around the campus of 1,000 students, the Holy Spirit was doing the same thing in every class — whether it was History, Speech, Bible, or any other. The faculty recognized immediately that God was visiting the campus. At noon the Dean of the college announced, "We will dismiss classes and go to the chapel for the rest of the day."

For three entire weeks, classes were dispensed with. Young people spent night and day in the chapel, sometimes as long as 48 hours, seeking the face of God. God moved in their lives. His Spirit swept through in waves of Glory! As you picture the wind sweeping over a wheat field; so you could see those young people being swept by the wind of God — like waves on a driven sea!

One afternoon at 1:30 as the Holy Spirit was sweeping through the student body, He swept down the aisle where I was kneeling and touched me, laying me flat on the floor. God's Spirit came down and picked up my Spirit and transported it out of my body. God transported me to heaven, then down Zion's hill to the cross-road of life, then down the broad road that leads to destruction. I visited the very gaping mouth of hell itself! In three and one-half hours, I received seven distinct visions which were to shape and form my ministry and life in the days and years that followed.

Now whether you believe in visions or not, is not my dispute. I would like to preface what I am about to share with this: When God gives a vision, you must understand God is giving that vision to speak a truth or to show a lesson to the individual with whom He's dealing. We should not try technically to pull a vision apart saying, "Well, I heard about this vision and it contradicted that vision," because in a vision God is speaking a message to that particular person's heart. He gives a vision so that person will understand what He's trying to get across.

So, in a vision one person may see Jesus with a long, flowing robe. Another may see him dressed quite differently. That does not mean it is

13

not the same Jesus. Details of a vision may differ from person to person. We are not dealing here with doctrinal things but rather with lessons God wants to teach us. Remember that as we approach this vision.

To expound a bit further, let me share this. While conducting a crusade, the Pastor of the church, after hearing the vision I am about to relate, handed me several slips of paper.

He said, "I've got to let you read these. I've carried them in my Bible for six years. A Lutheran friend who really loved the Lord gave them to me just before he died, and he said, 'May God use these to help somebody find the Lord'."

When I began to read them—to my amazement—it was exactly the same thing I had seen at the gates of hell. It made me convincingly aware that what I had seen was not fiction or fantasy, but God Himself trying to get a point across.

The Bible states: **"Where there is no vision, the people perish"** (Proverbs 29:18).

How then do we get a vision so that we do not perish?

Again, the word of God has the answer: **"And it shall come to pass in the last days, saith God, I will pour out of my Spirit upon all flesh; and your sons and your daughters shall prophesy and your young men shall see visions and your old men shall dream dreams"** (Acts 2:17) (See also Joel 2:28).

Therefore, the answer is **by an outpouring of the Holy Spirit of God.** *If God had not given me this vision when I was eighteen years old, Mr. Pegelow, a hopeless wino, would never have found a place in the Kingdom of God. Through this vision God showed me how to help Mr. Pegelow.*

I want to share with you portions of two of the seven visions I received that day in the chapel.

3

The Visions

As God's Spirit caught me away, He took me down what I understood to be the roadway of life. As I walked down the roadway, I came to a "T" in the road. It was not a crossroad, but a "T". I could go no farther in the direction I was going and a decision had to be made whether to go to the left or to the right. As I pondered, "Which way should I go?", I became aware that someone was standing beside me.

I looked to the right and saw a straight, narrow road which seemed to ascend higher and higher. The higher I looked, the steeper it became. My eyes spanned the road, searching for its end. As I looked almost straight up the side of the steep mountain, over its crest came the most beautiful translucent light I had ever seen. It looked so appealing. It looked so peaceful. It was the most glorious thing I had ever witnessed. The light seemed to quicken my mortal mind and body. I seemed to have an extreme amount of energy. I seemed totally able to express myself. It seemed that my entire being had expanded. I did not know where that road led or what was beyond that mountain peak, but I knew one thing for sure: when I got there, I'd be able to see where I was, the light was so brilliant!

Then my eyes were drawn away from the crest of the mountain, back to the "T" in the road. Looking to my left, I saw a very broad road, like a tremendous super highway. It appeared easy to travel. In fact so easy, it was "downhill" all the way! Farther along a large curve in the road almost made a complete circle. Eventually it became as a spiral staircase, winding ever downward. The farther my eyes swept down that road, the more I became aware of penetrating and absolute darkness, finally resulting in a total eclipse. I could no longer see where the road was leading. I could not see its destination. There was nothing but total darkness. When my eyes finally hit the darkest spot in the road, a shiver went through my entire body. It was eerie! It was deathly! My whole being was repulsed by the intense darkness I beheld.

Next my eyes were drawn away from the left road, back to the "T" in the road. I heard the one who stood beside me say, "Son, which way will you go?"

I said, "Well, there's no question in my mind. I want to go where the light is."

He said, "Son, come, follow me."

He led the way.

I followed. It wasn't long until the air became heavy and my breath became short. My brow filled with sweat, and my heart began to beat faster. My feet became leaden in nature and it became increasingly difficult to pick them up. Finally, as the road continued leading upward, I came to the point where I fell in exhaustion.

I said, "I can't take another step! My legs are too heavy. I have no breath. I can't go on."

The one who was leading the way looked back with tender eyes and said, "Son, why don't you lay down some of the things you are carrying?"

For the first time in this experience, I looked at myself, noticing that I was carrying all kinds of things with me. Looking over the inventory of all my possessions, I made a decision.

"I really don't need to take this thing along," I said. I laid it down. The moment I did, the sweat began to disappear, my heart began to beat normally, and my feet were once again light.

We started back up the road. But it wasn't long until my feet became heavy again; my heart began to pound; the sweat on my brow became intense. All strength seemed to be completely gone.

Finally I fell, and again I said, "I can't take another step."

Again those tender eyes looked back at me and he said, "Son, why don't you lay something else down?"

Looking over the remaining inventory, I discovered something else that really did not need to be dragged along, so I laid it down.

He said, "Fine. Come, follow me."

Once again my breath was normal, my strength returned and my feet were light as a feather. This procedure continued as we progressed up the mountain. Time and time again I fell beneath the load. Yet each time I surrendered one more thing, I found myself able to go on.

> *I am not going to elaborate on what "things" were left along the road. You must know, however, that as I struggled along, each item was clearly identified. Some were possessions, some were attitudes, some were activities. It required laying down things I loved which were not evil but which consumed a great deal of my time. To be sure, the*

items would be varied and/or in a different order for each of us.

In this life there are many weights and sins that can easily beset us. As we walk the roadway of life with Jesus Christ there comes a time in our lives when we need to lay some "things" down.

"Let us lay aside every weight, and the sin which doth so easily beset us, and let us run with patience the race that is set before us" (Hebrews 12:1).

Finally I came close to the crest of the mountain. The roadway appeared to rise straight up. Falling beneath the load one final time, I looked up at that insurmountable mountain and said, "There's no way I'm going to make it. There's just no way to walk; the pathway is too steep."

Have you ever opened the Bible, looked into God's Word and said to Him, "It's impossible for me to do that?" Well, that's what I said to God right then.

He said, "Son, why don't you just lay down the last thing in your life?"

Amazingly, at this point, there was only one thing left in my possession! My reaction was, "Well, I've just got this **one thing left,** let me keep it."

"He said, "Why don't you just lay it down? You won't have need for it when you get to where you are going."

I looked at the light and knew if I could reach that light I would have everything I'd need. In the illumination of the light, the thing I was still carrying became insignificant.

I was able to say, "Well Lord, I don't need this either."

The moment I laid the last thing down, it felt like my feet were not even touching the ground. In an instant, I rose up over the crest of the mountain. What had once seemed an insurmountable peak, I reached with ease, in the twinkling of an eye. When I reached the top of the mountain, I was bathed in the bright translucent light. Before me was the most beautiful city eyes could behold.

In that magnificent city, scenes passed like a motion picture before me. I have been around the world and visited in many of the nations. I have seen many of the wonders of the world, but there is nothing nor any place in the world that can compare with what I saw. There are many details about the glorious splendor of this city I could share: the streets of transparent pure gold (Revelation 21:21), the Glory of God lighting the city (Revelation 21:23), but details defy description, as the very nature of God permeated every space and every breadth of the city.

"And he carried me away in the Spirit to a great and high mountain, and showed me that great city, the holy Jerusalem, descending out of heaven from God" (Revelation 21:10).

What a joy to understand Jesus' words in John 14:3 **"And if I go and prepare a place for you, I will come again and receive you unto myself;**

that where I am, there ye may be also."

As we walked through the gate, the one beside me led the way to the most elegant banquet hall I have ever seen. Not one famous building that mortal man has ever built would compare to this banquet hall. When I walked inside, the scene almost took my breath away! The splendid crystal and china, the sparkling silver and chandeliers - I had never experienced anything so magnificent in all my life before, and I've been treated on occasion to some fabulous meals in fancy restaurants. There were tables so long it seemed you could not see the end of them. The kitchen where the meal was being prepared was beyond description. I tasted morsels that my tongue had never before tasted. Just one taste was enough to satisfy me, totally. The places at the tables were all set.

I was led by the one who was guiding me to a particular table. Then he took me to a specific setting. There I saw a nameplate with my name on it.

He said, "Son, as you follow me, you'll have a place in this great banquet hall."

My heart leaped for joy to know that I had my reservation in! Very soon, I became aware that the places on either side of where I was to sit had no nameplates. I looked down the table in either direction and there were no other nameplates anywhere near mine.

I said, "Why is my nameplate all alone here? Surely everyone wants to come to a place like this. **Surely** everyone is interested in being here!"

He said, "Son, that's why I brought you here. I want you to help fill these places."

I asked, "How can I do that?"

He returned a question, "Do you really want to know?"

I replied, "Yes, Sir, I really want to know."

He said, "Alright. Come, and follow me."

We retraced our steps down the aisle, through the door we had entered, and out of the beautiful banquet hall. He led me across the transparent golden streets sparkling so unbelievably pure, straight out of the gates of the city, and down that steep road we had come up. We ended up right back at the "T" in the road.

When we came to the "T", he took me to the left, that broad road. This time as I looked to where the broad road led downward into darkness, I was amazed to see things I hadn't noticed the first time. The road was filled with a river of human beings streaming down the highway. As I looked at this mass of humanity, I saw great anxiety written on their faces — frustration, confusion, perplexity. I could hear them rustling and pushing and shoving, always reaching, searching, hoping for something. It all seemed so urgent.

Sensing an urgency even within myself, I said to the one who was with me, "Why are all these people going in that direction? Haven't they ever been to the city from which we have just come?"

Shouting to the crowd, I cried, "Hey there, you don't want to go that way. **This** is the way to go."

The Visions

The drone from the mass of humanity seemed to drown out my voice. I lifted my voice to the top of my lungs, "Don't go that way! Go this way!" But the louder my voice became, the more intense their drone seemed to become.

Becoming frantic, I said, "I've got to do something about these people."

I reached my hand into the stream of humanity. It was like a whirlpool drawing me into its movement. Have you ever been on a road when a freight train or a huge semi-truck went by? You almost get sucked right under the wheels! When I got close to this stream of humanity, it would have been the easiest thing in the world just to fall in step with it. It took great effort to keep my equilibrium. I braced myself! I didn't want to go with them!

As I reached into the stream again, I grabbed a man by the arm. He turned and looked at me cynically, his eyes like cold steel. He shook my hand off his arm as though I were a snake biting him.

Instinctively I said, "Sir, you don't want to go that way! Come, go the way I've gone."

He turned around and with those steel eyes snapping said, "Mind your own business, Kid. I'm going to go my own way."

Immediately, I reached for other persons. There were many different reactions from these people. I grabbed some with such insistence I'm sure it hurt them. Most of them didn't say a word, but their eyes almost withered my hand as I touched them. **Every one** of them shook my hand loose as their unflinching eyes indicated, "Leave me alone."

Finally, filled with frustration and anxiety, I cried, "What can I do? How can I help these people?"

Then, the tender Shepherd who had been leading me said, "Son, do you really want to help them?"

I said, "Yes! Oh yes, I do!"

Once more He said, "Come, follow me."

Do you know where we went? Right down the roadway that led spirally into darkness - down, down, down - through bitter blackness.

The Visions

As we rounded the last spiral on the road, the darkness seemed to split wide open, like curtains being opened on a stage.

Suddenly before me was a scene like a state fair or a huge carnival. Lights were glaring and flashing; the music was jolly, hilarious, titillating; barkers were crying out about their wares. The stream of humanity I'd traveled along with quickly branched out, standing and gazing at the sights before them.

It was as if at that moment they had to make a decision in their lives. Not everyone in the stream of humanity was brash; many were bashful and backward and undecisive, but it seemed they were all being forced to make a decision as to what they would most enjoy.

The exaggerated sensuousness of the whole scene was unbelievable. There was every type of allurement and enticement imaginable. Everything that would gratify the appetite, everything to satisfy the body, everything to stimulate the mind — it was all there. Absolutely everything and anything ever conceived was available.

Mr. Pegelow

Situated all around were salesmen who, anxious to sell, were barking about their wares like carnival men enticing us into a side show. People were agape at all that was offered. Many stood there not knowing what to take. Others seemed to know what they wanted. I could see their eyes light up. I could see their bodies begin to respond as they picked out the very thing that was the "apple of their eye." As soon as the choice was made, they would follow the salesman to a counter, lay down their money, go through a turnstile, on through a swinging door and could no longer be seen. I watched as the more shy, undecided ones were trying to make up their mind about what they wanted. Soon one of these sly salesmen would spot them also.

"Hey, bring your friend over here. I want to show you something," the enticing salesman would encourage.

Pretty soon that shy, backward person, who didn't know how to make up his own mind, had someone "helping" him.

"This is the thing you want to try," and the salesman cleverly would give his pitch to show them the benefits of his particular allurement.

Well, some were still undecided. I watched the vendor bend down to the person and I moved closer to hear what was being said.

The salesman would say, "Hey, if you'll just try what I've got, I'll make a deal with you: I'll pay your way in if you'll come through my turnstile."

Satan's operation, as the enemy of our soul, has a way of "helping" us get started down his roadway. If he can't get us to pay our way to start, he'll pay the way for us just to get us hooked. But we'll "pay" somewhere down the road. He knows before he's through with us, he'll get all our riches anyway. When somebody tells us how to make an easy buck, we usually end up in a trap. Contracts and dotted lines usually follow free gifts. Know this! Whenever we disobey God and go the way of our own desires, we are only fooling ourselves. Someday we'll see things from God's perspective.

Finally, I saw those undecided people get sold on the devil's lie that he would pay the bill. Even those who couldn't convince themselves eventually were convinced by someone else. Each made up his mind and chose **something** and off he would go through the turnstile of life.

I said to the One next to me, "Where are those people going?"

He said, "Come, follow me."

He took me through a turnstile and the swinging door. We walked into a dimly lit room.

Once inside, we viewed another large banquet hall. The tables were long — as far as the eye could see. There people were seated, enjoying and partaking of the thing that had enticed them. As they came through the turnstile and swinging doors, they were led to the particular table which was their choice. Once they were seated, they were served what they had chosen. And it was exactly as they wanted! It was an eerie room: smoke filled; the lights were strange; the noises were weird (the most terrible I had ever heard). The smells were nauseating (the strangest I had ever smelled). It made the hair on the back of my neck stand straight up. It was like an accumulation of everything evil or that ever could be evil.

We observed the crowd. People were laughing. People were singing. People were going through all kinds of situations they thought was happiness. It seemed everyone, even the shy ones, got caught up in the revelry of the moment. They made merry until that which was given to them was consumed. As they desired more, they had to make a request for it and it began to cost them. Each time they were given what they wanted, they had to pay a little bit more money until finally all the money they had was gone. Still their desires were not satisfied. Once their money was gone, the scene would change. The waiters would take them a little farther back in the room as they begged and pleaded for more.

"I haven't got any more money, but I've got to have what I want."

The waiter would shake his head and say, "I'm sorry, buddy, you haven't got anymore to give."

"But," he said, "I've got to have some more. I'll give you anything. What do you want?"

The waiter bargained with him, "Alright, if you want it that badly, I want your job."

Each advance toward the back of the room, would strip them further of something that had once been precious to them in life. They all paid a price each time to get what they wanted. They gave up their jobs, their families, their health, their mentality, their own will. Until ultimately they were so hooked that they had absolutely nothing to say about what they were going to give up, but were easily pliable in the hands of the waiters.

Finally, as they reached the last table, I noticed something. When these persons who had sold everything (including their souls) to satisfy their desires, when they had nothing else to give (their own will entirely depleted), the waiter would then look to the end of the banquet hall. I looked down the smoke-filled room, and saw a throne upon which sat a very sinister-looking man. A man with the look of greed and lust in this eyes and a slight grin on his face (more like a sneer) occupied the throne.

He seemed to be saying, "This is my operation and I've got these people where I want them."

I watched the man who sat upon the throne. Later, I learned it was the Devil himself. Those waiters and emissaries were his demon powers reaching out for souls. As a waiter would look up, the one on the throne would wink his eye.

Later, I learned the book of Proverbs says, **"He that winketh with the eye causeth sorrow"** (Proverbs 10:10).

In general, I've discovered, when someone winks his eye, he's got something mischievous and destructive on his mind, and what is gain

*for the winker usually costs an inno-
cent party. Do you agree? Think
about it the next time you go to wink
your eye!*

Well, I learned that Mr. Lucifer himself
uses the winking of the eye to give out his
orders.

Finally upon reaching a place of desperation
and attempting still to satisfy the lust of the
flesh, having given all they had to pay the
price for what they wanted, they were refused
any more.

Eventually in total abandonment they'd
say, "Well, take **anything.**"

They were hooked. It was worth the price,
they thought. Finally, as they approached the
throne in the back of the banquet hall, they
gave Satan the very last thread of their own
will. There was absolutely nothing left of
themselves at all. Satan completely cap-
tivated them by his will. At this point, the
waiter would stop and look to the throne. The
man who sat there with the cold eyes and
sinister sneer would wink his eye. When he

did, it was a sign for the waiter to maneuver that poor, completely-helpless soul through the final swinging doors. I watched the men and women and young people as the waiters took them and pushed them through the swinging doors. Soon after they disappeared, I'd hear a scream which would fade away into oblivion.

I turned around to the One who was with me and said, "Tell me, where are they taking these people?"

He said, "Son, come, and follow me."

We pushed the swinging doors open and I saw a precipice with a very sharp decline. I watched as people were pushed over the edge of that precipice. They would sink into oblivion and, when the area would light up, that would be the end of the person.

Turning around, I pleaded, "Please, we've got to do something about this!"

All of a sudden I stopped dead in my tracks. My heart nearly stopped beating. I looked up and screamed, "I **know** that man! I **know** that man!"

He said, "Yes, Son, you do know that man. That's why I brought you here."

I asked, "What are they doing to him?"

He answered, "Watch."

As I watched, I recalled that he was a man from my hometown. It was Mr. Pegelow, the man I had walked past time and time again. I thought he was just another silly drunk. I began to realize he was really just a defenseless creature who couldn't help himself. Mr. Pegelow worked for a junk dealer, right in the junkyard, disassembling pieces of equipment for the reuseable parts. Mr. Pegelow never shaved and he never cut his hair. He never even washed his hair; it was matted just like tar.

His body reeked with an odor that one could smell a block away. His clothes had not been off his body in months because on Friday night when he got his paycheck, he went directly to the bar, cashed it, and bought all the wine his pockets could hold. He took his wine bottles, put them in his pockets and went straight to the Milwaukee Road Depot steps. In the summer time, that's where he lived all weekend — on those steps. In the winter when it was cold outside, he went inside. Nobody touched him or even bothered him.

Mr. Pegelow came from one of the wealthiest families in town, but he was dubbed the "bad boy" of the family and everyone in his family disowned him. He thought the whole world had turned on him, so he turned to a bottle for a cave in which to hide. He thought no one cared for his soul.

In my vision, I saw Mr. Pegelow come to this precipice of life. I saw the wicked waiter take hold of Mr. Pegelow, weak and not knowing where he was going. He quickly pushed Mr. Pegelow over the side. I rushed to the precipice and looked down. As I looked, the eyes of Mr. Pegelow met mine.

His mouth did not say a word, but his eyes said, "Please help me! Please help me!"

I watched this man sinking, his eyes crying out to me. I couldn't take my eyes off him. As he sank into this pit of darkness, it split wide open and flames from an eternal furnace spewed out of the mouth of that gapping hole. Those flames, like arms, reached up and began to draw him into that furnace.

All the time, those eyes locked to mine, were saying, "Please help me!"

I looked down into those eyes and said, "Dear God, what can I do?"

And the One who stood beside me said, "Reach out your hand."

I said, "He's too far gone."

Immediately He said, "Son, **reach out** your hand!"

I answered, "I can't reach him."

Patiently He said, "Son, give him your hand."

Something inside me impelled my arm to shoot out and I reached over the precipice toward those eyes that were saying, "Please help me!"

When my arm was fully stretched out, I began to notice something happening. Mr. Pegelow's flight to the furnace was abruptly brought to a standstill. Immediately the gears reversed, and Mr. Pegelow began to come up out of those flames, back through the darkness. He got closer, and closer, and closer until I could feel the warmth of his flesh. My hand instinctively reached out and grabbed him and I pulled him up over the edge of the precipice. When his feet were planted on solid footing, the expression in his eyes changed. They looked at me and although he said nothing with his mouth, his eyes said, "Thank you! Thank you!"

The One who was with me came over and took Mr. Pegelow's dirty hair in his hands. He threw His arms around that filthy man, and embraced him. When he took His arms away, Mr. Pegelow was just like he had taken a bath. He was a brand new man — **a brand new man!**

> **"Therefore if any man be in Christ, he is a new creature; old things are passed away; behold, all things are become new" (II Corinthians 5:17).**

The One who was with us said, "Bob, follow us."

I followed the One and Mr. Pegelow right straight back through that rowdy banquet hall, through the turnstiles, past that hilariously boisterous mob and beyond the broad roadway of life. We climbed back to the "T" in the road. We proceeded to the road that led upward. When we arrived, Mr. Pegelow started climbing. I watched as Mr. Pegelow made it to the top!

When we all got to the top, we walked back into the Holy City. We walked to the elegant banquet hall. We came to the table where my nameplate was and the One who was with us said, "Bob, look at the nameplate next to yours." I did, and there was Mr. Pegelow's name!

There was a big smile on Mr. Pegelow's face and we sang the victory songs of Zion together.

4

Reality

Six months later I left Bible College to go back to my hometown. I had been home only four days. On Sunday evening, I was walking to church, across town from my home. When I reached the railroad tracks, on the west side of Grand Avenue, something caused my eyes to look over at the Milwaukee Road Depot. There sat Mr. Pegelow with his head sunk on his shoulder. Immediately the vision of six months before flashed into my mind.

I told myself, "I must do something with that man."

Mr. Pegelow

This was back in 1953. I was wearing a brand-new grey flannel suit. That was when the grey flannels were the "in" thing. I had on a white shirt and a black knit tie. My shoes were nicely shined and I was ready for church.

I walked over and said, "Mr. Pegelow?" and he mumbled, "Yeah?"

I tapped him on the arm and said, a bit louder, "Mr. Pegelow!"

"Leave me alone."

I said, "Mr. Pegelow, would you like to go to church with me tonight?"

Again, "Leave me alone."

I looked up and breathed a prayer: "God, what am I going to do now? The man's drunk. I don't know what to do with him."

Then I remembered: "Reach out your hand; give him your hand."

So I said no more. I just reached down, got my shoulder in the shoulder socket under his arm, and took his dirty arm and wrapped it around my white shirt collar and my grey flannel suit. When I lifted up that arm, there was no need to worry about cockroaches or anything else because they couldn't have lived there. If you've ever picked up a person who is drunk, you know what kind of dead weight that can be. When I stood erect, I found that he was shorter than I and that made additional trouble. But I got his arm around my neck and my shoulder in place. Somehow I pulled him along, half-way on his feet and half-way dragging him.

Now, my church was located on the other side of the heart of the city from my home, and I had to walk down Main Street, past all the stores. Since it was Sunday evening, not too many people were on the streets. When I got about half a block down the road, to where the bar was, where Mr. Pegelow always cashed his check, I heard a car pull up beside me.

Somebody rolled down their window and said, "Hey there, what are you doing with Mr. Pegelow?"

I stopped dragging the man and looked up into the face of a burly policeman!

Now everyone knew who Mr. Pegelow was but not too many people remembered who I was.

He asked again, "Hey, what are you doing with Mr. Pegelow?"

I answered, "I'm taking Mr. Pegelow to church."

He said, "To church? A man like that, in that condition?"

I said, "Yes Sir, if you don't mind."

He said, "More power to you," rolled up the window, and went on.

When we got down by the J.C. Penney Store, a second squad car pulled up.

Another policeman yelled to me, "Hey there, what are you doing with Mr. Pegelow?"

Again explaining, "I'm taking him to church."

We'd gone about three blocks and still had about twelve to go.

He said, "Would you like a lift?"

Welcoming his offer, I said, "Man, yes, I would like a lift!"

He said, "Get in the back seat and I'll take you. Where is your church?"

I told him and he drove us there. We got out and the policeman helped me drag Mr. Pegelow inside.

Church had already started; the song service was in high gear. The church could seat at least 600 people but like many churches on a Sunday evening, there were only about sixty people there. Since the preacher had already moved everyone toward the front, there were plenty of empty seats. We had the back all to ourselves. We sat down in the very last pew.

Only the pastor, the organist and the song leader saw us come in. But, do you know what happened? It wasn't long before people started turning around. It wasn't because they saw we were there. Possibly it was because they smelled something and were looking to see what that strange odor was. People who had once been drunkards themselves began to look. Quite a few years had gone by since God had rescued them. Now they were big business people and they no longer cared for anyone but themselves. They turned around (even the deacons) and gave me dirty looks. They didn't say a word, but their eyes said plenty and the sneer on their faces told me a lot.

The preacher gave his message. The altar call was given. The only thing I got out of Mr. Pegelow the whole service was "Where's my bottle?" or a snore. He was either asking for his bottle or sleeping just like a little baby.

Well, I knew nothing the preacher had said had gotten through to him. God **had said**, "Give him your hand." So when the altar call was given, I once again put that dirty arm around my neck and I pulled him to his feet. I dragged him down the red carpet in that brand-new $250,000 church. I made our way to the front, dragging him all the way. When we got to the altar I just dropped him and he

fell onto the beautiful carpet. I started praying and I prayed every prayer I knew how to
pray. Remember, I was just an 18 year old
boy. I said everything I knew to say. I did
everything I knew to do. All I could get out of
Mr. Pegelow was a grunt.

I said, "God, I've done all I can do. **You've**
got to do something to help me."

Motioning to my pastor, he came over. How
I praise God that he had the Holy Spirit in
him. He began to pray a prayer. All of a sudden something touched the pastor and he
started crying. Tears started to come from his
eyes as he got a burden for this man lying on
the floor. When the pastor started getting a
burden, something started happening in Mr.
Pegelow also. Mr. Pegelow started stirring
and moving around. I looked at Mr. Pegelow
and he was looking straight at me.

He said, "Where in the world am I?"

I said, "Mr. Pegelow, you're in church."

"How did I get here?", inquiringly.

I said, "I brought you."

Mr. Pegelow

"What am I doing here?"

Reassuringly I told him, "You are going to find Jesus as your Saviour tonight."

He said, "Nobody cares for me. Nobody loves me."

I said, "Yes, somebody loves you. God loves you and we love you."

As I watched his dirty old face, a tear came into the corner of his eye. That tear started running down his face and you could see a streak where the tear trickled as it washed the dirt away. Pretty soon the tears started on the other side of his face, and then the fountain of his deep began to break up and he began to cry a fountain of tears. My pastor who was broken with compassion knelt with Mr. Pegelow on the floor. He put his arms around him and began to console him and lead him to Jesus. It wasn't long until the drunken man was sobered up by the power of God. He was praying the sinner's prayer and meaning it from the depths of his soul. That once dirty old face began to light up with the glory of God and you knew something had washed that man whiter than snow.

> "Have mercy upon me O God..."
> "...Wash me and I shall be whiter
> than snow" (Psalms 51:1a and 7b).

To see the Lord working so mightily became electrifying to the sixty people who were in church that night. God began to deal with other hearts, and soon some of the staid, starchy deacons started to weep. Before long some of their wives were crying also. Eventually the whole place was in tears. Big, burly men came over and put their arms around dirty old Mr. Pegelow and got their white shirts soiled. As the smells and the dirt came off on them, they didn't seem to notice because the love of God was being transmitted directly to Mr. Pegelow through them. Surely the love of God covers a multitude of sins.

> "Above all things have fervent
> charity among yourselves: for
> charity shall cover the multitude of
> sins" (I Peter 4:8).

That night something wonderful happened in Mr. Pegelow.

My Dad, who was a deacon in the church and a businessman in my home town, came over to me. His bright blue eyes were covered over with tears.

He threw his arms around me and said, "Bob, whatever possessed you to bring Mr. Pegelow to church tonight?"

I answered, "God possessed me." I had never told him about the vision.

He said, "Bob, that's the best thing you could have done. I'm proud of you."

He went over and hugged Mr. Pegelow.

Presently, I felt someone squeeze my elbow. There was my Mom with tears running down her face. She said, "Bob, do you think Mr. Pegelow would like to come home with us tonight? I'll wash his clothes; he can take a bath; and we'll put him to bed for the night."

Looking at Mom, I said, "Thank you, Mom. I think he'll come. I'll ask him."

Well, when Mr. Pegelow heard that, he couldn't believe his ears and he just broke up all over, inside and out.

5

Angels Unawares

"Be not forgetful to entertain
strangers; for thereby some have
entertained angels unawares"
(Hebrews 13:2).

Mr. Pegelow went home with us that night.
Mom fixed him a plate of chicken; then she
got busy cleaning. Talk about a ring around
the tub! Mom had quite a few "rings around"
before the night was over. It took her several
washings and part of the night to get his
clothes clean.

That night was the first night in twelve
years that Mr. Pegelow had slept in a bed or

had a pillow for his head. He slept like a little baby.

When breakfast was ready the following morning, we had to awaken Mr. Pegelow. When he woke up, his first words were, "Thank you, Jesus."

Mr. Pegelow got dressed. He hadn't been in clean britches for a long time. When he took them off they could have stood by themselves, but now they fit just like a glove and he was ready to go to work, shining and bright, shaved and clean.

Dad and I took him to the junkyard and plumbing supply business in the station wagon and let him out. Curiosity compelled us to watch what would happen next.

Mr. Pegelow walked up the steps. At the counter was the boss's son, a fellow with whom I had graduated from high school.

When Mr. Pegelow took his time card out of the rack and put it in the timeclock, the boss's son called out, "Hey there, what are you doing? That's Mr. Pegelow's card."

Mr. Pegelow turned around and said, "Good Morning!"

The boss's son blinked his eyes and said, "Are you Mr. Pegelow?"

He said, "I sure am."

"What in the _____ (you can fill in that word) happened to you?"

Mr. Pegelow said, "Listen, **that's** what it's all about! I just got out of **that** place." Radiantly he went on, "I gave my heart to Jesus last night!"

Startling news travels fast in a town of 15,000. It didn't take very long for Mr. Pegelow's story to make the rounds. To confirm that the change in Mr. Pegelow's life was true, people would drive by the Milwaukee Road Depot. They found no Mr. Pegelow sleeping on the steps. He had rented a room and was now living at the local hotel.

6

The True Banquet

We made arrangements to pick up Mr. Pegelow after work on Wednesday so he could come to our home for dinner. We were going to take him along to Wednesday evening services.

Wednesday night at 5:00 o'clock, Dad and I drove up to the junkyard. We waited. Five minutes after 5:00 and no Mr. Pegelow. Ten minutes after 5:00 and still no Mr. Pegelow. Twenty minutes after 5:00 and still no Mr. Pegelow!

Dad said to me, "Bob, maybe you'd better go and ask if anyone knows where Mr.

Pegelow is. Maybe he left work early or something."

Jumping out of the car I went inside, "Hey, have you seen Mr. Pegelow? He was planning to have supper with us tonight."

The boss's son looked at me and said, "Bob, haven't you heard?"

"Heard what?"

He said, "Mr. Pegelow died today at 2:00 o'clock as he was working by the old magnet in the back of the junk yard. And do you know - the fellow who worked beside him said he heard him say, 'Jesus, I'm coming home'!"

I stood there and wept as I threw up my hands and said, "Thank you, Lord." Someday Mr. Pegelow is going to pull up his chair next to mine at the great marriage supper of the Lamb and I'm going to meet him again on the other side of this life.

> "...Blessed are they which are called unto the marriage supper of the Lamb" (Revelation 19:9).

There we will sing the victory songs of Zion together and we will forever be in that glorious light.

> **"And the city had no need of the sun, neither of the moon, to shine in it: for the glory of God did lighten it and the Lamb is the light thereof"** **(Revelation 21:23).**

7

The Acceptable Time

I have shared with you a vision from God, that you might get a vision for the people who are around you. Right this moment, on the block where you live, down the road from your house, on the job where you work, in the school where you learn, in the place where you shop, you are passing people like Mr. Pegelow every day of your life. They live in a cave of their own existence and they feel like no one loves them or cares for their soul. Or perhaps you yourself are feeling like you're trapped. You feel you're bound by things which you are not able to lay down. You feel you lack the strength to go on. Many people, young and old, can identify with what Mr. Pegelow was going through. The longer you continue to go that particular way, the worse it will get. I'm sure of this one thing: hell is a real place which you want to stay away from. Don't wait until you get to the precipice of life. There might not be anybody on the precipice to reach out a hand to help you. Jesus said:

> "Behold, I stand at the door and knock. If any man shall hear my voice and open the door, I will come in to him and will sup with him, and he with me" (Revelation 3:20).

Today is the accepted time — the day of salvation.

> "Behold, now is the accepted time; behold, now is the day of salvation" (II Corinthians 6:2).

If you feel like the world is bigger than you and it's caving in on top of you, you can do something about it. Jesus was sent into this world to rescue you. Just tell Him, "Jesus, I feel like a lost person. I'd like to be found. I'd like to be rescued. I need help. I accept you this very moment as my Lord and Saviour."

Or perhaps as a Christian you would like to confess, "Jesus, I know I lack the vision I need for the lost souls around me. I pray that God will pour His Spirit upon me and give me a love for others, that I might begin to be concerned about the people I pass every day. Help me to share Jesus with them so they may also be at that glorious banquet hall."

I trust you will never forget Mr. Pegelow at the gates of hell. With God's help, you will recognize that it could be the man down the street, the person you work with each day, a loved one in your own family, even yourself, needing rescuing off that broad way that leadeth to destruction (Matthew 7:13).

It's really not hard to help people, if you are sincere about it. When you really love someone, you can help them because love is a language everyone understands. I like to picture Mr. Pegelow, redeemed, with the great cloud of other redeemed witnesses cheering us on:

"Wherefore seeing we also are compassed about with so great a cloud

of witnesses, let us lay aside every weight, and the sin which doth so easily beset us, and let us run with patience the race that is set before us, looking unto Jesus the author and finisher of our faith; who for the joy that was set before him endured the cross, despising the shame, and is set down at the right hand of the throne of God" (Hebrews 12:1 and 2).

I can picture Mr. Pegelow, a voice in that great multitude, singing:

"Alleluia, for the Lord God omnipotent reigneth. Let us be glad and rejoice, and give honour to him: for the marriage of the Lamb is come, and his wife hath made herself ready" (Relevation 19:6b and 7).

"And the Spirit and the bride say Come. And let him that heareth say, Come. And let him that is athirst come. And whosoever will, let him take the water of life freely" (Revelation 22:17).

Discount Schedule

Books	Less	Each	Shipping
1-9		$1.25	$2.00
10	20%	1.00	2.50
25	30%	.88	3.00
50	40%	.75	5.00
100	50%	.63	10.00
200	60%	.50	12.00

Specify English and/or Spanish

JUBILEE DESIGN
112 Horseshoe Dr.
Burnet, TX 78611-5919
512-756-7321
goodmon@tstar.net